BLUNDESTON
THEN AND NOW

Olwen Offord
Ken Blacker

**A photographic record of changes over the
years in a Suffolk village**

**Blundeston and District
Local History Society**

INTRODUCTION

This book commemorates 40 years of the Blundeston & District Local History Society and illustrates, through photographs old and new, many of the changes that have taken place in our Suffolk village between the latter part of the 19th century and the present day. It is not intended to be a concise history of Blundeston, but merely tells the story of the homes and businesses of some of the villagers who have lived here over the years. In common with countless other villages up and down the country, Blundeston has transformed with the passage of time from a lively, self-contained community supporting a whole host of trades, into an almost purely residential village with no shop or post office, requiring all goods and services to be bought in from outside. Despite this it still remains a very pleasant place in which to live.

We are indebted to many villagers who have loaned us photographs which have been scanned and added to our Society's collection, some of which have been used in this publication. Most of the modern day photographs have been taken by the authors themselves, and we are grateful to the Lowestoft Journal for giving permission to publish the last photograph on page 60. Some of the photographs are not as sharp or clear as we would have liked, but they are of historic interest and have been included when no better alternatives have been available.

Much of the information accompanying the photographs has been derived from censuses, directories or press cuttings, but also from historical publications such as Alfred Suckling's "History and Antiquities of the County of Suffolk (1846)", and also from our Society's two detailed publications dealing with Blundeston village history. We are particularly indebted to Trevor Wright, who now lives in Driffield but whose ancestors lived in Blundeston. His meticulous research from a variety of original sources has proved invaluable to the authors in piecing together much of our village history.

At the time of publication we believe the facts quoted within the book to be correct, but as we have already discovered with earlier volumes which the Society has published, mistakes can happen while subsequent research sometimes throws up new knowledge which changes earlier perceptions. The authors would be pleased to receive any new information which comes to light as a result of this publication and to learn of any inaccuracies which may have inadvertently occurred. We hope the book will provide enjoyment to all those who read it and that it will perhaps stimulate greater interest in one of Suffolk's pleasantest villages.

OLWEN OFFORD
KEN BLACKER

ISBN 978-0-9955354-0-4

Blundeston & District Local History Society
Tranquil
Hall Lane
Blundeston
Suffolk NR32 5BL

Printed in Lowestoft by Olympic Print

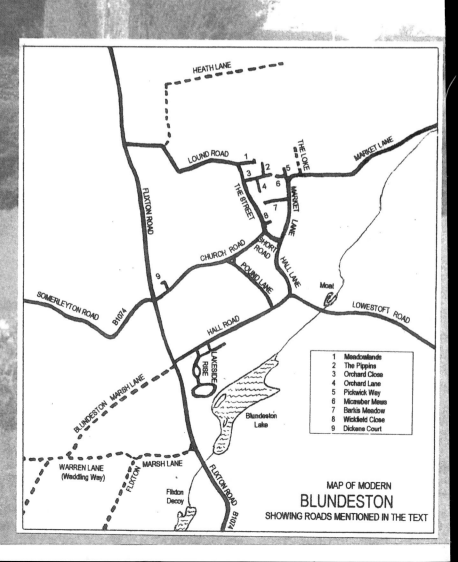

1	Meadowlands
2	The Pippins
3	Orchard Close
4	Orchard Lane
5	Pickwick Way
6	Micawber Mews
7	Barkis Meadow
8	Wickfield Close
9	Dickens Court

MAP OF MODERN
BLUNDESTON
SHOWING ROADS MENTIONED IN THE TEXT

CONTENTS

FLIXTON MARSH LANE

The ancient and still unsurfaced Flixton Marsh Lane remains to this day a remote and little visited part of Blundeston. **Warren Anne** is the most westerly residence in Blundeston; beyond it the track along Wadling Lane leads to Blundeston Marsh which, since May 1847, has been crossed by the Lowestoft to Norwich railway line. **Warren Anne** is a very old property which could date from the 17th century. In 1805 James Barber was the owner/occupier of this yeoman's farmhouse with 21 acres of land. By 1850 it had become a public beer house called Warren Arms owned by Frederick Morse, a Lowestoft brewer and local landowner. Later it became a farm cottage and in 1884 was sold to Sir Savile Crossley and became part of the Somerleyton estate.

The occupants of the cottage from at least 1911 and right through the inter-war period were Ernest Gissing, a cowman, and his family. Ernest died on Christmas day 1970. **Warren Anne** was sold into private ownership in 1971 and was subsequently enlarged at its northern end by Mike Reeder in traditional style. The photographs show **Warren Anne** as it appeared in 1937 and as it is today.

Blundeston covers over 1600 acres of land including arable farms and marshes. The farm in Flixton Marsh Lane was originally called Warren Farm and is shown as such on the 1805 map, and it later became known as **Decoy Farm** In 1837 the farm was owned by the Morse family who were important landowners at the time but in the 1870s/1880s it was sold and became part of the Somerleyton estate. It was farmed by generations of the Collen family from at least 1892 until 1971 after which Lord Somerleyton sold the farmhouse and buildings but kept the land.

The aerial photograph shows **Decoy Farm** in 1970, the farmhouse itself being the white-painted structure on the left. This large impressive building remains basically unaltered in external appearance to this day. The large thatched building at the centre of the site is the old barn. All the former stables, cow sheds and storage buildings were removed from in front of it when it was converted into houses, but the original outline of the old barn is clearly visible from the photograph taken in 2014

FLIXTON ROAD

Gray's Oak Photographed in 1937, these three old cottages stand almost opposite Flixton Marsh Lane. The two larger ones were renovated in 1938, which was probably when the house nearest to the camera was demolished. They later became a single dwelling on which total renovation commenced in about 1996, and the second photograph was taken just before this work began. Their appearance has been much improved by the removal of the rendering to reveal the brickwork. In its current form the cottage is named **Gray's Oak after** a pollarded oak tree nearby under which Thomas Gray, author of 'Gray's Elegy', used to sit when visiting his friend the Revd. Norton Nichols at Blundeston Lodge.

It is hard to believe that, a little over a century ago, this rustic highway was what is now the busy B1074. A fully laden horse-drawn cart ambles along a leafy Flixton Road past the long low thatched cottages which in 1837 were owned by Joseph Chapman of Blundeston House and were lived in by Thomas Wright and Samuel Beckett. Both may have worked at the 'Big House'. The Osborne family subsequently lived here for many years but by the 1960s the cottages had become derelict and in 1972 were virtually demolished and replaced by the modern house which, in a nod to its past heritage, is called Old Thatched Cottages.

In the years before the internal combustion engine came into regular use, wells and ponds were essential sources of water for villagers and for farmers and their animals. Most of the ponds which once existed in the village have now been filled in, but Peto's pond, at the junction of Flixton Road with Church Road, still survives. The only time it was ever recorded as drying out was in the very hot summer of 1976. For many years this pair of old farm cottages stood in Flixton Road facing Peto's Pond. They also belonged to Joseph Chapman and were in existence at the time of the 1837 census when they were lived in by Eleanor Brown and William Flatman. The adjacent field was then known as Brown's Close. The cottages were demolished in the nineteen-sixties, leaving no trace that property had ever existed on this site. In 2011 a new traffic layout was installed to improve safety at the adjacent road junction.

Peto's Barns   These barns, also owned by Joseph Chapman, later became part of the Somerleyton Estate. By the nineteen-eighties they were disused and decaying, but planning permission was granted to convert them for residential use. Work began in 1993, and the exterior structures of some barns – including the largest one – were preserved. Other buildings, such as the former pigsties, were demolished and replaced by new dwellings but using the original footprint so that, overall, the original appearance of the group was retained. In the yard behind the barns a small estate of large detached houses was built and called Dickens Court. The photographs show the original barn complex, the interior of the largest barn with the roof removed in October 1993, and the completed houses in 1996 before foliage grew up to obscure the view of them from Flixton Road.

CHURCH ROAD

Blundeston House is the tallest and most impressive residential structure remaining in Blundeston. Nathaniel Rix of Oulton commissioned Sir John Soanes to design the house which was completed in 1786, replacing an earlier building on the site. It is in Italian style and comprises three floors and a basement. The external brickwork was originally painted white to reflect the Italian influence. The house and it accompanying estate was bought by Joseph Chapman in August 1834 from the Revd. Edward Missenden Love, with further additions purchased from the Revd. Love in October 1838 and from the Revd. George Anguish, owner of the Somerleyton estate, a year later. Chapman later moved to The Laurels in Oulton, and Blundeston House was let out for while, one occupant being the Revd. Robert W. Cory before he moved to the parsonage in Blundeston, but by 1851 the house was unoccupied. Chapman's death resulted in the sale of his Blundeston property to Samuel Morton Peto in October 1852. It appears to have survived the disposal of the Somerleyton estate by Sir Samuel in 1863 with ownership remaining in the Peto family. Sir Samuel's nephew Lawrence Peto, a Lowestoft estate agent and Justice of the Peace, had moved in with his family by 1890. He died in December 1938, and after his widow Henrietta died in September 1946 the house and its immediate grounds were sold to Stanley Rudd who ran a haulage business and a market garden from there for about two decades. This view of **Blundeston House** is taken from Church Fields Path and shows that, despite modern renovations, the exterior remains true to Soane's original design.

This map of Blundeston and the surrounding area is believed to date from about 1850; it certainly post-dates 1847 as it shows the railway crossing Blundeston Marsh. **Blundeston House** is named on it as High House and later in the 1800s it was known as The Lawns. The position of the farm workers' cottages at the nearby road junction is also shown on the map, as are Peto's Barns. In addition to the road layout which is familiar today, a number of other roads are shown, such as the one leading past Warren Farm to Somerleyton along the ancient Wadling Way, which were never subsequently paved and in many cases have now deteriorated from well-trodden routes down to little-used tracks.

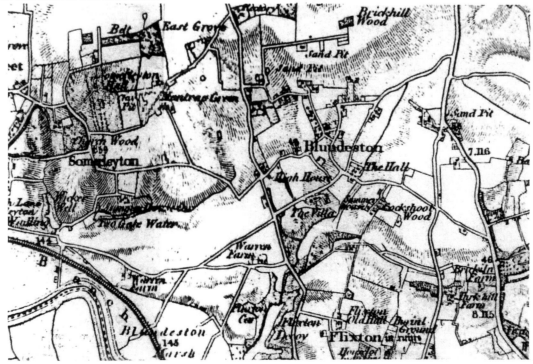

Blundeston School   In 1726 the Reverend Gregory Clarke bequeathed land to endow a school and teacher for "twelve poor scholars".   It is not known exactly when the school was constructed, but by 1829 its condition had deteriorated so badly that it had to be rebuilt.   In 1850 an additional classroom was added on the other side of the master's house and built to the same height as it.   The wife of an early master, Owen Hastings, is buried in the next door church yard, as is another master, Charles Chaston Fiske.   This photograph was taken in about 1900 at which time the school could accommodate about 100 children.

Structural defects and overcrowding became ongoing problems, and in 1929 the school was completely remodelled to the form shown in this photograph which was taken in the 1960s.   The master's house was eliminated, allowing the school to be enlarged by some 16ft, and the headmaster moved to a chalet bungalow in Hall Lane.   It could now accommodate a roll of 185 pupils.

During World War II a hut was erected in the school grounds for the use of the Home Guard which passed into school use when the war ended.   It was augmented in about 1947 by this prefabricated HORSA hut which provided two extra classrooms for practical subjects.   The HORSA (Hut Operation for the Raising of School leaving Age) scheme was a nationwide initiative to provide schools with additional buildings as a short term (10 year lifespan!) measure.   The Home Guard and HORSA huts were both built on the school field alongside Church Road. The Home Guard hut was demolished in 1965 and the newer hut in about 1986 when the school was again remodelled.

This aerial view shows the school in the 1990s. A reception classroom was added in 2005. Educational restructuring by Suffolk County Council meant that two extra year groups had to be accommodated by the provision of additional administrative and classroom facilities in 2010. At the start of 2015 the school roll stood at 191 pupils.

The **Church of St. Mary the Virgin** photographed in the early 1900s. . The oldest part of the present building is the tower, the lower part of which is Saxon in origin. There is also evidence of Norman construction in the church. The nave was extended southwards in the 14th Century leaving the tower asymmetrical to the body of the church. The narrow, crenellated tower, which tapers inwards towards the top, is notable for its height at 54ft. It holds two 17th Century bells both of which were renovated in about 2004. The upkeep of the church and its grounds is today the responsibility of the parish.

The entrance to **St. Mary's** from Church Road as it was in the 1940s and as it is today. The old sundial is believed to be the one to which Dickens referred in *David Copperfield*. It fell from its mountings in the 1980s and a new one now correctly indicates the time. The old wooden doors of the porch had been replaced by new wrought iron ones by the 1980s.

A modern view of **St. Mary's Church**, as seen across the field from Pound Lane, shows the large east window which dates from a major reconstruction carried out in the 1850s Most of the side windows originate from the 14th and 15th Centuries.

Inside **St. Mary's**. Fourteen large oil lamps were bought in 1897, making it possible to hold evening services. They were removed when electric lighting was installed in 1932. Additional lighting was added when the church was rewired in 1982. The middle photograph, taken in 1983, shows the Victorian floor tiles, most of which were broken and could not be re-used when they were lifted for the installation of underfloor heating in the nave in 1985, although those in the chancel were retained as this was not included within the new heating system. At the same time the old pews at the front of the nave were also removed but these were recycled within the church, some to make a permanent wall for the vestry. The new concrete floor was originally covered with rush matting, but carpeting was subsequently installed in 2008/9.

The handsome **War Memorial** was erected in the church grounds in 1921 to commemorate local men who gave their lives during the First World War. It lists thirty names, to which a further seven were added a quarter of a century later in remembrance of those from the village who were killed in World War II.

The Village Pound. As early as the 16th Century each village or township would have had its pound, an enclosed space where stray animals were kept pending reclamation by their owner. On some maps of the 1800s the Blundeston pound is shown as **Pinfold**, an alternative name used in some parts of the country. In charge of each pound was the 'pinder', who was responsible for looking after the animals and would collect a release fee when an animal was claimed by its owner. The pound is now a little remembered aspect of our rural heritage, but fortunately our one in Blundeston is still complete and in good condition, and stands as a defiant reminder of the past at the top of Pound Lane at its junction with Church Road. The pound was the last item of property within the village owned by the Lord of the Manor, and funds were raised locally for its restoration in 1959.

Ninety years or more probably separate the first two photographs, both taken from the same spot looking towards St. Mary's Church, during which time Church Road has become a well-used thoroughfare.

When viewed from Pound Lane the entrance doorway can be clearly seen. In the background, on the site of a former pond, stands the village sign erected in 1963 by the Women's Institute to celebrate the organisation's Golden Jubilee. Designed and carved by Leon Bradford, it depicts a young David Copperfield leaning on an arch framing the church. Photographed in 1993, the pavement in front of it has just been built to complete a continuous footpath between the village and the school.

The **Old Rectory** in Pound Lane is renowned in literature as the house which Charles Dickens chose as the birthplace of David Copperfield in the novel of the same name which was published in monthly instalments in 1849 and 1850. Architectural features of the house suggest that parts of it may date from the 16th Century, and a building is shown on the site in the 1783 map. Rectors of the parish used it as a parsonage from at least the 1840s and the heyday of the house was under the Reverend Robert F. Cory between 1882 and 1925. It was awarded Grade 2 listed status in November 1954 because of its Dickens connection, and was described at the time as "18th century with a late 19th century service range at the rear".

By 1969 it had fallen into such a perilous state of repair that the rector moved to a new bungalow in Market Lane. In 1975 the house was sold by the Church Commissioners to Frederick Mayzes who renamed it **The Rookery** and finally moved in with his family in 1981 after six years of restoration work. The external renovation was very sympathetic, and a comparison between photographs taken in the 1920s and the 1990s shows how unaltered its appearance has been.

Hopefield in Church Road was a much more modest dwelling and was the home for many years of Sidney Cooper whose father had been the last member of the Cooper family to live and work at the mill. Sidney lived in the bungalow and used the large shed as a warehouse to store household goods, paraffin etc, which he sold around local villages, first of all using a horse and cart and, later, a van. He also bred and raced pigeons and had a large loft for them in the garden. He died in April 1990 at the age of 97, and later the bungalow was enlarged incrementally out of all recognition while a new house called **Jonway Lodge** was built on the old 'warehouse' site. A feature of the much rebuilt **Hopefield** is the splendidly ornate brick chimney which graces its eastern wall. The photographs of **Hopefield** contrast how it looked in 1990 with its appearance in 2014.

A small **Methodist chapel** is known to have existed in Church Road since the 1810s but its exact location is not known. In October 1869 Mr. Heaver sold three adjoining cottages to be converted into a more substantial chapel. The building was adapted to include a gallery and could hold 80 people. Congregations increased, so a larger purpose-built replacement was erected in The Street and the old one closed in 1909 but continued to be used as a reading room, meeting room and store. The date of this photograph – which shows the mill sails in the background – is unknown.

The building was converted in 1942 for use by the Auxiliary Fire Service for the duration of World War ii, and a door was inserted at the front to allow access for two large cars which pulled the fire pumps. In 1947 the Suffolk & Ipswich Fire Service took over and the door-way was enlarged to accommodate the modern Commer fire engine shown here. The fire station closed on 31st March 1974 when the service was transferred to Lowestoft.

During the war an air raid siren was installed on a tall pole outside the fire station which, in peace time, was used as a fire siren. For many years the building has been used as a piano showroom and workshop, but in 2012 work began to convert part of it back to a private dwelling. This work was ongoing when photographed in early 2015.

Nos 3-5 Church Road. In 1837 these cottages were described as 'tenements' owned by James Cleveland, who owned the whole plot up to and including the smithy o the corner of The Street. Cleveland had other premises in The Street itself where he ran his wheelwright's business. One of his tenants in the cottages was William Scurrel a boot maker. In this wartime view a Home Guard contingent marches past, presumab on the way to their hut in the school grounds. The blacksmith's forge is out of sight behind the taller house (East Dene), and the village post office was also located there in the later 1800s prior to moving to a new location in The Street.

The post office was run up to about 1892 by WilliamHenryWaller who afterwards stayed on in Blundeston as a journeyman joiner. His brother, Walter John Waller, was also a postmaster - at Somerleyton - before buying a grocery and draper's business in The Street, Blundeston.

Across the road at its junction with The Street, can be seen (top photograph) the end of the terrace of old houses known as **Ellen Cottages.**

The boot making tradition continued for many years, and well into the 20th Century Ted Flaxman made and repaired shoes at this hut in the grounds of his house at **no. 3, Elstow.** He was there when war started in 1939 and died in November 1955 at the age of 72. In the 1990s the now-disused hut was moved a short distance away to no. 1 Ocean Cottages and a new house, **Meadow View,** was erected on the site.

Elstow is nearest the camera in this 2014 view. Front gardens have vanished to accommodate parked cars, and in the distance Ellen Cottages have given way to a new terrace of houses built by Lothingland Rural District Council to replace the old ones which were demolished in 1968/69. On the other side of the tall house, **no. 6 East Dene**, is now situated a modern detached residence at no. 7 where the blacksmith's shop and post office once stood.

The Glebe comprised an extensive piece of arable land adjoining the Rectory which had served as a benefice for successive clergymen for several centuries. A view taken in 1993 shows the old fire station and Elstow amongst the buildings fronting Church Road while, on the far right, are some of the shallow-roofed council houses in Short Road erected in the 1940s and designed by local architects Tayler & Green. The Norwich diocese owned this land but after negotiations part of it was designated as an 'open space' in 1979. After submitting plans, the Parish Council bought 3½ acres of **The Glebe** in 1998 to establish a Millennium Green.

Local people were involved in designing, clearing and planting the site under the guidance of the Suffolk Wildlife Trust. Jill Blacker, John Blowers and David Jermy are seen tree planting in December 1998. At the time the back of the old Rectory could be clearly seen across the remaining section of glebe land, but by the time of the February 2015 photograph the trees had become so well established that they hid this view The **Millennium Green** was inaugurated when the beacon was lit for the first time on New Year's Eve 1999. The young oak trees planted in a circle around the beacon were still only small when they were seen peeping above the snow in January 2003 but they are now maturing well.

FURTHER ALONG
FLIXTON ROAD

In the mid-1850s this section of Flixton Road was called
Lound Lane.   Situated in an exposed position alongside the
roadway, with no protection from the bitter easterly winds
blowing across the open fields behind, was a pair of old and
damp farm workers' cottages which in 1837 were owned by
Joseph Chapman and inhabited by George Reed and John
Norton.   Living conditions were primitive with an outside shed
for a toilet and another containing a tin bath.   In early post-
war years the cottages were rebuilt and became a single
dwelling complete with running water and electricity, and also
with the reputation of being haunted.   By the end of 2001 the
old house was empty, but the old outbuildings behind it still
remained.   It was subsequently rebuilt and greatly extended
to form the attractive **Thula Cottage** that fronts Flixton Road
today.

The tithe survey of 1837 shows **Flowerlands** as belonging to
William Rudd whose extensive landholding included a nursery
ground and adjoining arable land.   The modest one-
bedroomed house, set well back from Flixton Road, was later
expanded with an additional bedroom in the adjoining barn .
Extensive greenhouses once existed to the right of it, and
attached to the main property at right angles were two small
cottages facing onto Lound Road, but these were demolished
in the 1950s.   By 1891 the market gardener at **Flowerlands**
was William Morris, who was succeeded by Charles Bailey,
and the market garden remained in the Bailey family's
ownership until his son George retired in 1970.   Today the
barn at **Flowerlands**, and many other buildings have gone.
The house is now a private residence but the core of the old
dwelling remains within the much altered domestic property.

LOUND ROAD

The old smokehouse at **The Homestead** in Lound Road.   In times gone by there were a number of smokehouses in Blundeston, which is no surprise in view of its fairly close proximity to the sea.   Fishing was once a major occupation for villagers, and in the 1871 census no fewer than 23 men and boys from Blundeston were recorded as being employed in the Lowestoft fishing industry.   Several local men lost their life at sea.   It would have been natural for fishermen to bring some of their catch home and for some of it to be smoked for sale to other villagers.   The smokehouse at **The Homestead** was one of the last two in Lound Road until it was pulled down when the house was being renovated in about 1995.

Charles Batchelor (or Batcheldor), a carrier and coal merchant from about 1892, lived at **The Homestead** by 1911 and possibly earlier.   In 1912 he was recorded as running daily into Lowestoft and he also served Great Yarmouth on Wednesdays and Saturdays.   Like many village carriers of the time, he probably mixed passengers and merchandise together in a dual purpose vehicle.   He retired in about 1925 and died in January 1939 at the age of 76.   By 1939 **The Homestead** belonged to market gardener George Fisk, and in about 1951 Walter Jermy of Poplar Farm bought the property and built greenhouses on the land adjacent to the house.

Poplar Farmhouse.   The 1768 map shows the land on which **Poplar Farm** now stands as part of Blundeston Common, but by 1805 there were buildings on the site.   Brick rubble, which is presumably the remains of these, has since been found north of the existing domestic complex.

Poplar Farm was farmed by Alfred Waller and then Palmer Rivett but owned by John Owles and his two sisters.   After John's death 111 acres were sold to Sir Savile Crossley for £3,500 and he had the present farm-house built in 1900.   In 1919 102 acres were sold to sitting tenant Palmer Rivett for £3,600. Walter Jermy became the owner in 1927 and **Poplar Farm** still belongs to the Jermy family.

Two photographs show the farmhouse as originally built, and as seen in 1996 with modern extensions, before a mature tree screen had developed to hide the view of it from Lound Road.   The cottage on the left, known today as **Portland**, was originally two semi-detached dwellings probably built in the 1850s or 1860s which marked a time of expansion in Blundeston when the number of families in the village grew from 158 to 183.   In 1939 one was occupied by Arthur White, a carpenter and agricultural wheel-wright, and the other by Arthur Vincent who ran a radio and cycle shop in The Street.

No. 2 Raglan Cottages. Little is known about the two properties known as **Raglan Cottages** which probably date from the middle of the nineteenth century. The modern photograph, taken in 2014, shows that the long front garden is still as luxuriant as it was about 90 years earlier, but the elderly widow pictured in the earlier scene, Emma Tripp, would scarcely recognise no. 2 now as, like its neighbour, it has since doubled in size. She lived there alone, her 12 children having all left home, but was not isolated as a daughter and grandson still lived in the village and a son lived in Flixton. Emma Tripp died in 1922 at the age of 90.

Norwich Cottages comprised a terrace of cottages with a smokehouse at the far end. They faced the footpath linking Lound Road to Church Road, and had long rear gardens. They are shown in the 1837 tithe survey as belonging to Robert Purdy with William Bultitude and others (unnamed) quoted as tenants. William was drowned at sea in 1841 aged 29, leaving a widow Susan and two young sons. A much later tenant was Lambert Ward who lived at no. 5 and operated the smokehouse. He cycled around the village selling herring, bloaters and kippers until the time of his death in 1950 at the age of 67. The cottages, which had only very basic facilities, were demolished in the late 1950s and a single bungalow, Keinette (now renamed Navan) was built on the site.

Beyond Norwich Cottages is **North View**. The colour photograph was taken in 2003 since when the enclosed front porch has been removed during renovation works. The long shed, which earlier stood alongside the footpath, was used from about 1925 onwards and throughout World War II by Cecil Osborn who ran a business from North View as a pork butcher and poulterer, and was renowned for his tasty sausages. From about 1937 he was also a dairyman, using a pony and trap to deliver milk to Ashby and Lound.

In the middle of the nineteenth century this area of Blundeston was referred to as North End. **Blue Gates** (formerly known more prosaically as no. 7 Lound Road) was set well back from Lound Road and is thought to be one of the oldest in the village. It was built by Robert Shuckford and was lived in by the Manship family in the 1830s. The next owner was John Owles whose widow sold it to its existing tenant, shoemaker Levi Rudd, for £145 in 1891. It remained in his family until 1995 when his daughter Mabel (Hathaway) died, having lived in the cottage for the whole of her 94 years. She was photographed in her 91st year at the end of the path leading from Lound Road to her cottage.

Blue Gates has since been extensively renovated and modernised. Today it is called **Wishing Well Cottage** after the well that still remains as a feature of the garden.

Cobbler's Cottage is on the right hand side of the two properties photographed in 1991. It was built on Plough Common and appears on the 1842 map when it was owned by the Goffin family. Its present name indicates the trade of long term resident Arthur Horne. Arthur formerly lived at Norwich Cottages, and local carpenter Herbert Wright made him a wooden shed in which he worked. He took this with him when he moved, and continued to use it until he retired from his position as the last remaining cobbler in Blundeston, although latterly the old hut was barely recognisable because of all the ivy growing on it.

Arthur Horne died in 1995 after which a new owner completely remodelled and greatly extended **Cobbler's Cottage** whilst taking care to use matching brickwork. The small cottage to the left of it, **Pentuan**, is believed to have been built onto Cobbler's Cottage in the mid-1800s.

Windy Ridge stands on land which was once part of the Somerleyton estate, but it was later owned by Stanley Rudd who used it as an orchard before local builder Horatio Taylor constructed the house on it for Wallace Benstead, probably in the 1920s. Wallace followed his father in the trade of saddle and harness making, which the family had pursued in Lound Road since 1891, though Wallace was working on his own by 1901. He had a large wooden shed erected at the side of the house by local carpenter Herbert Wright from which he conducted his business. Wallace died in August 1938 aged 67. With the spread of mechanisation to farming and to transport generally, the need for new leather goods diminished and the hut later became dilapidated and redundant. This was the view in 1993.

In 2015 **Windy Ridge** still looked much the same as it had always done apart from the fitment of new window frames, and it had been in the hands of the Forder family for about three quarters of a century. However, to the west of it things have changed. The old harness-maker's hut was demolished in 2007, and the unnamed cottage beyond it, latterly part of Poplar Farm, was pulled down in 1997 to make way for the substantial new property **Boyton**.

Situated towards the front of a property which in the1830s had been part of a large tract of arable land owned by the trustees of John Spence and known as Woods Close, was a sprawling wooden bungalow called **St. Quentin**. In the 1940s and 50s Mrs. Lilian Harold cut hair here and also had a small cigarette shop. Reached via a narrow driveway between the adjacent properties of The Bungalow (now renamed Paddock View) and Melita, little of **St. Quentin** was latterly visible from Lound Road because of all the mature foliage surrounding it. This wooden property, and its ramshackle garage, were subsequently demolished to make way for a large new bungalow erected in 1975. The name **St. Quentin** was retained for about 20 years, but it is now known as **Woodlands**.

Melita replaced an older house belonging to the Goffin family in about 1800. A long term occupant for more than 40 years up to 1878 was bricklayer John Cooper, and it was only in his final years that a young niece joined him to act as his housekeeper. It was purchased in 1878 by Francis 'John' Offord who built a smokehouse at the back and in about 1900 extended the main house by joining it to its neighbour. The extension included a shop on the ground floor for Offord's china and glass business. By 1911 **Melita** was occupied by Noah Wright, a retired Company Sergeant Major and village postman, and his wife Julia Neta Wright ran an upholstery business from there which she continued after Noah died in 1929 aged 61, at which time she purchased the property. Her son, Herbert, constructed a shed in the garden from which he worked as a carpenter. All commercial activity there had ceased by the time Julia Neta Wright died in February 1970.

In 1991 the property, which up to then still had no bath or inside toilet, was extensively modernised to combine the house and shop into one unit, but the smokehouse was retained at the rear – although it had probably not been used for its original purpose for almost a century – and it is now the only one remaining in Blundeston.

The Laurels was built on a site which in 1837 was owned by Samuel Rounce and consisted of arable land, a cottage (since demolished) and a garden. By the 1860s it was owned by William Rivett, and in the late 1800s Arthur Middleton, a Blundeston shoemaker, paid £250 for it. The Laurels was probably built in the early 1900s. The 1933 Kelly's Directory described William Rushmere as a shopkeeper there, and on his death later that year his wife took over the business and was subsequently succeeded by her daughter Freda. Freda ran the shop as a general store until she was rushed into hospital in August 1987 when it closed, never to re-open. Subsequently the house and shop were sold as a private residence. Due to the distinctive shape of the building, the photograph of **The Laurels** taken in 2015 does not take too much imagination to picture the shop as it was in earlier days.

THE STREET

The Street is Blundeston's main thoroughfare and represents the heart of the village. Back in the 1800s it was frequently referred to as High Street and occasionally as Mill Street. At the time of the 1837 survey it was built up on the western side only as far as where the Red Lion stood until quite recently, while across the road there were no properties north of the old blacksmith's shop. Nothing else existed until you reached the cluster of residences at what was then called North End except the pair of old semi-detached low-roofed cottages where The Street turns sharply left into Lound Road which were formerly known as Rose Cottage and Wentworth House but have now been converted into a single dwelling. On The Street itself, almost all the domestic properties lay on the western side; apart from Ellen Cottages and the Mill House, there were only two other residences on the right hand side, the rest being taken up by the mill itself, a large brickworks, and a blacksmith's shop.

The track leading straight on from The Street at its junction with Lound Road goes to Common Farm. As early as 1783 the map shows buildings on the farm which may have got its name from the old Plough Common, much of which appears to have been appropriated for farm use. In 1837 it was owned by the Woods family of Blundeston Hall from whom James Rounce bought it in 1912. The 73 acres were sold to Walter Jermy for £1,725 in 1933. This painting by Paul Sargeant shows the farm buildings in the 1960s; they were replaced by modern prefabricated ones in 1972.

The old view, believed to have been taken at about the time of the first World War, shows the extent to which housing had then spread. On the right hand side a rudimentary pavement reaches as far as Framsden Cottages, which are set back and just out of sight of the camera. The cottages on the right of the photograph are **Vicot** and **Blades Cottage**. Once known as **Norman Cottages**, they were built by Samuel Norman on land belonging to Sarah Wicks who, until her death in 1891, owned much land to the west of The Street. Behind the hedge in the left foreground was an extensive plot of charity land controlled by Blundeston Church-wardens and rented out as allotments.

In the 2015 photo many of the same houses are still identifiable but the cobbler's shop standing side-on to the street has been swept away to permit the construction of Orchard Close, and across the road a gap in the building line has appeared with the demolition of the Red Lion

The date shown on the gable end of nos. 70-76 The Street is 1854, and from at least 1891 to 1896 no. 70 served as Joseph Curry's grocery and drapery shop. He is probably the man posing proudly outside his premises with female members of the family outside the front door of no. 72. In those days both formed part of a single property. Curry was succeeded by Walter John Waller who ran the shop until at least 1933, and later also sold hardware and paraffin for lamps as well as his customary range of goods. He was closely involved in the building and running of the Methodist Chapel further down The Street. The business later passed to Mr. and Mrs. Gage, and when they moved to the old fish and chip shop further along the street nos. 70 and 72 were converted into two separate dwellings.

This row of cottages was built on land formerly owned by Gidney Booth. He farmed a 15 acre plot between The Street and Market Lane until his death at the age of 65 in June 1870 but presumably found it profitable to sell The Street frontage for housing development.

The industrial style premises next to no. 70 were used by James Coleby, a boot and shoe maker and repairer, who had arrived in Blundeston from Lowestoft with his young family by 1871 and worked here until he was in his sixties. His son Albert gave up his position as licensee of the Red Lion to succeed him. Albert died in March 1936 aged 66 and his son Gilbert Coleby is recorded as continuing the business. The family lived next door to their cobbler's shop at **no. 68 The Street**, and for many years, Albert's wife Hannah ran the village telephone exchange from her front room. Hannah died in October 1962 at the age of 92.

Above Local ladies Mrs. Horne and Mrs. Grice with Walter Waller's shop in the background.

Left A 1995 view of no. 70 on the corner of Orchard Close. This new road was created to serve the 1960s housing and swept away the cobbler's shop and other outbuildings formerly on the site. No. 70 has been a hairdesser's under various ownerships since at least 1966. The small building at the back served briefly as a post office and general store for a while in 1991 but is now in private use. Since its closure Blundeston has lacked the post office service that it enjoyed for some 150 years.

Blundeston underwent a spell of major expansion in 1960s, about a century after its earlier period of growth but on a much larger scale. This aerial view highlights the start of this expansion, with the new houses of **Orchard Close** and **Orchard Lane** under construction in 1965. An extension of this development, **The Pippins**, came in 1968, while in 1968/69 the large rectangular meadow at the top of the photograph, known as Rivett's Midder, was swallowed up by the construction of **Barkis Meadow**. Finally the large area of allotments at the top of The Street where it turns sharply left into Lound Road (the latter hidden by trees in this photograph) was sold in 1970 for £9,600 and the money received was invested in Blundeston Charity Funds. **Meadowlands** was built on the site in 1971.

The bungalows of Orchard Lane are seen nearing completion in 1965 with the larger properties in Orchard Close visible beyond, while the view taken half a century later depicts the same properties within a now fully mature urban landscape.

Many old houses and cottages still survive in **The Street** although, with the passage of time, changes have inevitably been made to modernise them and also, in many instances, to enlarge them with extensions at the side or rear.   Some changes have been subtle and have preserved much of the original character whilst, in other instances, the modifications have been such as to leave the property almost unrecognisable from its earlier appearance.   Typical examples shown here embrace three adjacent properties which, like nos. 70-76, occupy land once owned by Gidney Booth but were built slightly earlier and were all occupied at the time the March 1851 census was carried out.

(Top) As recently as 2003 **no. 66 Twynham** still retained much of its original rather gaunt appearance, but today it presents a very different face to the world.   Only the right hand chimney stack remains unaltered from earlier times. *(Centre)* **Windsor Cottages (nos. 62 and 64)** still looked very much as-built when photographed in 1964, and even today no. 64 retains much of its original character.   The old name board still survives. *(Bottom)* **No. 60 Killarney** (since renamed **Yew Trees**) also retained much of its original appearance in 1992.   It is thought that the building at the side of the house was a carpenter's shop at one time, and in 1939 the house was occupied by Thomas Allerton who was night telephonist at the nearby exchange.

The **Red Lion** was a prominent feature in **The Street** and a major focal point of Blundeston social life for more than 175 years. The earliest known photograph of it is this one taken in the mid-nineteen thirties when it was owned by E & G Morse of Lowestoft. Morse's were taken over by Morgan's of Norwich in 1936 and their crown brewery in Lowestoft was closed. It is not known who the gentleman on the BSA motor cycle is.

The opening date of the premises as a beer house is uncertain, but its first licensee was shoemaker Henry Welton who owned the property at the time of the 1837 tithe survey. Initially the pub was called the **White Lion** and it is not known when or why the colour was changed. Henry Welton was still licensee in 1851, but by 1858 James Osborne had taken over, and in the years that followed many others were in residence with at least twenty more licensees recorded during its long history. The best known in recent times were Doug and Jan Penny who took over in January 1985. After Doug's death, Jan remained there until May 2009.

At one time there were stables and other outbuildings along the southern side of the property, and in the 1930s fish, meat and clothes were sold from one of these. A small brick building near the front was used as an ARP post during the second World War and it was later used as a men's hairdressers on Monday evenings. There used to be a mounting stone at the front for horses, but all these features were removed in the 1960s to enlarge the car park.

Several local clubs were based at the Red Lion, but it closed in November 2010 and in May 2012 an application to build houses on the site was approved. The photographs depict the **Red Lion** as it appeared in January 1993 with a pink frontage; the pub in its final cream-fronted appearance in December 2001, and during its demolition in August 2013.

The Nook at no. 46 The Street is best remembered as a fish and chip shop, but for most of the 19th century it served as a blacksmith's under the ownership of the Boyce family. William Boyce (born 1803) is the first recorded master blacksmith to work here. Subsequent generations of the family carried on the business until the last William Boyce gave up in about 1908, probably as an admission that two blacksmiths were more than a village the size of Blundeston could support. The premises became a fishmonger's, firstly with Robert Ward and later Leonard Ward, but in 1933 William Nicholls was recorded there as a fried fish dealer. In 1937 Mrs. Caterina Parravani and her sons, of the well-known ice cream family, took over and began manufacturing ice cream on the premises as well as selling fish and chips. On the outbreak of war trading ceased when Mrs. Parravani was required to move away from the coastal area because of her alien status while her sons were called up for active service. Fish and chip sales were later resumed, but ceased in 1972 when the premises became a private residence.

On the left of the top photograph are the old shop premises as they appeared in 1992. Their demolition in 2002 revealed a cobbled floor which had probably been the working surface for the old forge. The centre left view shows **The Nook** and the adjacent footpath to Market Lane as viewed across the derelict site which was the last piece of the one-time Gidney Booth land fronting The Street that still remained undeveloped. A large house (no. 52 The Street) has since been built on it overshadowing **The Nook**.

The former stable block was adapted many years ago with a blue roller shutter door enabling it to house a motor car, although it seldom did so. After the old stable was pulled down in 2003 a detached house was built on the site.

The bottom photograph, taken in 2007, shows **The Nook** after the old house had been renovated, with a new low wing adjoining it occupying part of the space where the old shop had once stood.

By the end of the nineteenth century the congregation had grown too large for the **Methodist Chapel** in Church Road and a search began for a new, larger premises. A site for the construction of a new chapel in The Street was offered by William Boyce almost opposite his blacksmith's shop. This meant demolishing two cottages, both of which stood end-on to the roadway. One was lived in by Boyce himself and had been the family home for many years. The other house was owned and occupied in 1837 by widow Sarah Wicks, who also owned several areas of arable pightle alongside The Street. The Wicks family had been related to the Boyces by marriage since December 1794, and by 1871 the residents were spinster Philis Wicks, a dressmaker, and her older sister Sarah Read.

In 1901 fifteen trustees were appointed to organise the building of a new chapel, and in 1903 a Mr. Cockrill was asked to draw up plans for it. Fourteen tenders were duly submitted for its construction and the job was awarded to A G Beckett for £757. A stone laying ceremony was held on 7th October 1909; a Certificate of Worship was issued on 11th December 1909, and the new chapel opened for services on 10th February 1910. With a large Sunday School room incorporated at the back, the final cost was £1,009.9s.0d, The old chapel in Church Road was sold in 1911 for £55. During the First World War the schoolroom was used as a billet for troops and the photograph was probably taken during that time.

As early as 1911 the new **Methodist Chapel** began to exhibit structural problems, particularly with water seepage. The front of it was later reconstructed to a far less ornate design with a much lower profile, completely altering its appearance when viewed from The Street. In this form it was used not only for worship but also for yoga and judo classes and for First Aid lessons, and also by various organisations such as the Ist Blundeston Brownies, the Young Farmers' Club, and the Youth Club. The large schoolroom at the back proved particularly useful for all these functions, and also for coffee mornings and other fund-raising events. This photograph shows the **Methodist Chapel** as it appeared in 1980.

The spacious and welcoming interior accommodated the large congregation on rows of pitch pine pews, and each seat had its own little metal fitting and name card. Lighting was originally by oil lamps suspended from the rafters, but electricity was later installed.

By the start of the 21st century the congregation had dwindled to fewer than ten, and the inevitable news came in 2001 that the **Methodist Chapel** was to close. The final coffee morning was held on 19th May of that year, and the last service was held on 24th June. Some contents had been in the chapel right from the start such as the pitch pine pews which had cost £35 when new and were sold for £1,000. A clock which had been donated in memory of E J Horn in 1922 was still working.

By the time of closure the back of the premises – the schoolroom and the garden beyond – were looking very neglected. The photograph inside the schoolroom was taken during its final fund-raising function in May 2001. Despite the extensive rebuilding, the damp problem at the front of the chapel was never cured, as the photograph taken in its final days of use shows.

The redundant chapel was sold in November 2001 for £110,000 and permission was obtained for two houses to be constructed on the site. Demolition was completed by March 2002. This photograph shows, on the far left, the first of the new houses nearing completion at the end of January 2003; today it is aptly named Old Chapel House. Further along the snowy street can be seen the Red Lion, itself destined to be demolished just over a decade later.

In years gone by many villages had a bakery and Blundeston was no exception. It is not known when Frank Jones started his bakery business next door to his house at **41 The Street** but it appears to have been well established by 1928. **Jones' Bakery** gained a reputation for the high quality of its bread, buns and cakes, and won a number of prizes for its Hovis bread. Frank Jones died in May 1933 aged 59 and his wife Charlotte carried on the business, and it later passed to her daughter Connie and son-in-law Arthur Runacres who continued to trade under the name of F J Jones.

A subsequent owner, Harrison Barker, converted the bakery ovens to oil firing, but competition forced him to sell to Matthes' large "Sunshine Bakery" in Gorleston. Matthes closed the Blundeston bakery in 1966, and it was demolished in 1970.

A photograph of September 1928 finds Frank Jones outside his bakery next to a fully laden cart with "Kitty" between the shafts and young helpers Jim Barrow – on the cart – and James Forder. The distinctive front of the Methodist chapel is just visible beyond the house next door.

George Codling, Frank Jones' head baker, is seen with a trade bike outside the building which had been Boyce's blacksmith shop in the 19th century. A smart Ford 8 car – Frank Jones's perhaps? – stands outside **41 The Street**.

In the bottom photograph, all traces of commercial activity had long disappeared from **41 The Street**, when it was photographed in 2014 with 41A next door, occupying the space where the bakery once stood.

George Codling stands at the entrance to the bakery with Philip Osborn and James Forder on the cart which has presumably just arrived back from making deliveries. The ivy-clad house across The Street, facing the bakery, had been owned many years earlier by Robert Goffin, a carpenter and master wheelwright. The Goffin family was in Blundeston for about 120 years, and other members of it lived in Lound Road. The house shown here is believed to be the one constructed by local builder Benjamin Jackson for a Mr. Goffin in 1822 for £23.7s.0d. The tithe survey of 1837 records it as a 'house, shop and garden' owned by Robert Goffin, who remained there until his death in June 1870 aged 78.

The Goffins' old house survives to this day and now forms the core of two greatly enlarged residences, **Anchorage** and **Jasmine Cottage.** The positioning of the two chimneys is now all that remains to give a clue as to the extent of the original property when viewed from The Street.

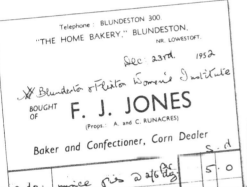

An overview of the southern end of The Street taken in 1965 with some of the prominent buildings marked. The photograph was taken a year before Jones' Bakery closed down and seven years before the fish and chip shop shut for the last time.

The passage of time is emphasised by these two views of **The Street**, both taken from exactly the same spot but with more than a century separating them.   We have the owner of the shop, Henry "Fiddler" Durrant to thank for the earlier photograph; he is the one with the stiff collar, dark suit and bowler hat, and his shop is just visible behind him.   Clearly an enterprising man, he produced a series of picture postcards of Blundeston which he presumably sold in his shop and elsewhere, and those that still survive provide a wonderful record of Blundeston as it was in the first decade of the 20th century.   "Fiddler" Durrant was clearly a self-publicist, and he featured quite prominently in several of his own photographs.

Many changes have taken place between 1908 and now, and yet many familiar landmarks still remain.   All the houses that appear in the early photograph are still recognisable in the later one, which was taken in May 2015, although the properties adjoining the shop on both sides have since changed in shape and size, and the substantial detached villa called **Lyndhurst** now sits between today's numbers 31 and 35.   On the left, the brand new houses on the old industrial site now hide the tower of the mill from view, which has been without its sails since about 1930.

Today pavements now line the roadway on both sides and the motor car is king of the road, but fortunately horses still trot up and down **The Street** quite often thanks to the nearby riding stables, and cycling is still enjoyed by many.

Because of its distinctive shape, there is no hiding the fact that no. **27 The Street** was once a shop. The domestic part of the property is very old and may well have originally formed two separate dwellings when it was built, probably in the late 18th or early 19th century. At the time of the 1837 tithe survey it was owned and occupied by James Cleveland and was described as a "house, shop and garden". Cleveland was a carpenter and wheelwright, an occupation inherited from his father Groves Cleveland who lived – probably in retirement – in property which his son owned in Church Road. The present distinctive shop frontage is thought not to be the one that existed in 1837 but a later construction. James Cleveland died in December 1879, and by 1902 the premises were occupied by Henry Durrant who had taken over from William Waller and his wife as postmaster. The photograph shows Mr. and Mrs. Durrant and one of their children outside the shop in about 1910.

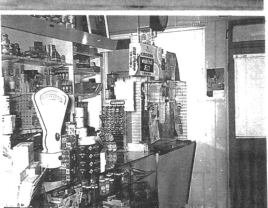

Henry Durrant had worked as a draper's assistant in London before coming to Blundeston. He ran the shop and post office for several decades, and it was probably during his time that the old property received a new roof and the dormer windows were removed. He was superseded in the war by Ted Gissing who kept the business going during the difficult early post-war years but sold it in March 1954 to Tom Lynch. The latter partly adapted the shop to self-service and considerably modernised the living accommodation. A subsequent owner, Mr. S A Arnold, who took over in March 1974, arranged for the traditional red telephone box to be re-sited away from the property to Orchard Close in 1976, where it remained until it was replaced by a characterless modern version in 1989.

Subsequent owners of the post office and shop were Tony Chilton in 1982 and Graham Wade in 1988. Graham was a baker, but despite the introduction of freshly cooked bread and cakes, the shop was unable to keep up with the growth of supermarkets and changes in shopping habits and it closed on 17th August 1990. The property became residential accommodation with the former shop used as a dance studio.

Holly House at 30 The Street would have been a very fine and substantial residence at the time it was built by Benjamin Jackson to replace an earlier property as his family residence. Jackson, who had followed his father Thomas into the building trade, employed four men, and he owned an extensive site from which he excavated clay to make his bricks and tiles. Benjamin Jackson died in July 1862 aged 66 leaving no offspring to continue the business which, along with **Holly House**, passed into the ownership of Samuel Norman. Trade continued to prosper, and by 1871 the number of staff employed had doubled and now included four boys as well as four men. Directory entries show Samuel Norman as still in business in 1904, but he died in August 1906 at the age of 71 bringing the history of brickmaking in Blundeston to an end, although his widow Louisa and daughter Catherine continued to live in the house for a few more years.

By 1935 **Holly House** was owned by Ernest Edward (Ted) Gissing and now served as a small shop selling sundry groceries and sweets from the front room. There was a cigarette machine outside and up to 1942 a petrol pump stood in the front garden. When Mr. and Mrs. Gissing moved across the road during the war to take over the post office, **Holly House** passed into the ownership of Colonel Norman and once again became a private residence.

As the photograph taken in November 1995 shows, **Holly House** and its adjacent plot were well tended and retained much of their old country village ambience. But two decades later the premises were in dereliction. In 2015 work began on renovating **Holly House**, and construction of a detached house on the adjacent garden was completed in the following year.

Benjamin Jackson's large brickyard site extended from Holly House to the mill and stretched for some distance back from The Street towards Market Lane. By the mid-1800s a kiln and various associated buildings could be found on the site, and clay excavations resulted in falling land levels, some of which can still be found in the area today.

After Samuel Norman's death the site remained largely derelict for many years, although in the 1950s Ted Gissing's son Eddie converted part of it to a cycle speedway track for village youngsters in line with a popular craze of the time. Some levelling took place in the early 1960s using surplus soil from the Blundeston prison construction site, and the **Blundeston Service Centre** was opened for car sales and servicing and the sale of fuel.

A 1982 view of the garage entrance shows the 'Shell' sign displayed prominently next door to **Holly House**; in subsequent years the fuel sold there was supplied by 'Fina' and was finally sold under the 'Little David' banner. For a short while in the early 1990s a small general store was operated from the premises, but by 1993 the garage business had closed and, as seen in the bottom photograph, the site was put up for sale.

Walton Garage bought the defunct garage and operated a well-equipped vehicle recovery and repair centre from **20 The Street** for a number of years, but subsequent to their removal to the industrial estate at Oulton all the buildings were demolished in 2011 and preparations began for the construction of a small housing estate. Most houses within the estate are on the newly constructed **Wickfield Close**, although – as this 2015 photograph shows – two of the new properties face The Street itself.

Country Cookin'. Ted Gissing had been doing a local milk delivery round from his shop in The Street since 1947. When he sold the shop in 1954 he retained the milk business and had this building with refrigeration facilities constructed on his land. He later sold the milk business to Long's Dairies of Lowestoft and his son Peter converted the building into a butcher's shop. Robert Fairclough continued the butchery business, but when Graham Wade bought the shop he branched out under the title of **Country Cookin'** and sold a wide range of groceries including his own baked bread and cakes.

In 1988 Graham moved to the post office at 27 The Street and Brian King began a business specialising in goods and services relating to water sports. During the 1990s the building was remodelled and enlarged. It is seen below under the banner of King's Watersports & Leisure. To the left, the now derelict land of the former garage business is being cleared for redevelopment. King's closed the water sports business in 2014 and the property was put up for sale.

The prices on Robert Fairclough's bill (below) make interesting comparison with those of today. It was probably issued in 1971 as the columns are in pounds shillings and pence although the sums entered on it are in the new decimal currency.

One of Blundeston's most visible landmarks is the old **windmill** at the southern end of The Street which, though long ago shorn of its sails, is a historic feature which we are fortunate to retain.

The substantial brick-built **mill tower** and the accompanying **mill house** were constructed by the Jackson family in about 1820 using their own bricks made from clay excavated from the pit behind the mill. The tower, which tapers inwards to a diameter of 14 ft. at the top, was fitted with patent wooden sails and equipped with a pair of French millstones to grind the corn. Benjamin Jackson's younger brother John was shown as proprietor of the milling business, but his tenure as miller does not appear to have been totally successful. On 25th May 1841 the mill and dwelling house, along with a granary, stables, cart sheds, and a ½ acre garden with fruit trees, were auctioned at the Crown & Anchor Tavern in Lowestoft High Street with Benjamin Jackson acting as contact for the family. His brother John was described as "retiring from business" although he was only 38 years old at the time. Reading between the lines of the sales literature, it would appear that the mill had been allowed to fall into a poor condition, but it had been put right and was described as "now in a good state of repair".

The auction was advertised to "Millers and Capitalists", and the purchaser was Thomas Cooper, a 24 year old from Southtown, Great Yarmouth, who was destined to remain at the mill until his death in September 1907 at the age of 90. Some of his sons joined him in the business as they grew old enough to do so, and it prospered to the extent that, by 1855, the Coopers had added a bakery to their other activities. After Thomas Cooper's death milling and baking continued under the title of 'Cooper Brothers' in the hands of sons Henry and Arthur. The last known record of them as millers was in 1916 but they continued to be shown as bakers up to 1925.

The mill house and the defunct mill were sold to timber merchant Abbey Beare who, in about 1930, removed the sails from the mill but retained the cap to preserve the brickwork of the tower. When Patrick Paul purchased the mill house in 1951 he found that he had also acquired the mill tower, and upon his retirement in 1981 he renovated the brickwork and re-capped it, designing all the replacement components himself including the weather vane.

The photograph shows the mill house in November 1995 including the low-roofed kitchen which was replaced by new owners after Patrick Paul's death in 2002, and at the same time the main house was substantially renovated. In 2011 new houses were built in the garden on the low level site of the former clay pit.

Cooper's invoice to C M Leather Esq. indicates a massive £89.16s.4d owed in February 1906. Hopefully the Coopers had customers who paid more promptly than Mr. Leather amongst their clientele!

The first beer house in The Street was opened in the early 1800s by William Bristow – known as Barney – a brewer and maltster at **The Malt and Hops**. He grew hops in the garden and brewed beer on the premises. By 1851 one of his eleven children, Alfred, worked with him and by 1855 had succeeded Barney as licensee. By 1864 Robert Rounce, a bootmaker by trade, was the licensee, and by 1881 his granddaughter Louise and her husband Henry Taylor were living with him, with Henry Taylor recorded as running the business by 1888. At an unknown date – possibly when Robert Rounce took over from Barney Bristow – the name was changed from **The Malt and Hops** to **The Crown Inn**. Unlike the Red Lion and the Plough, **The Crown** did not undergo a succession of managements and was in the ownership of just two families for more than a hundred years.

Henry Taylor was clearly a very versatile man, for in addition to running the pub he traded as a carpenter, and another string to his bow was the manufacture of coffins in pursuance of his third role as village undertaker. He appears to have served in this capacity almost to the time of his death in October 1939 at the age of 88.

In addition to being a pub, **The Crown** was used at various times as a meeting place and as a doctor's surgery, but is best remembered as the place where Blundeston Women's Institute was first established at a meeting on 26th January 1922 under the guidance of Mrs. Arnold of Blundeston Hall. The single storey annex was used as a shop from at least 1922 when Henry Charles Taylor was established there as a cycle agent.

The Norfolk brewers, Lacon's, appear to have been connected with **The Crown** by the nineteen-thirties, but they ceased to be involved in 1937 and Kelly's trade directory for that year shows it as no longer in business as a pub. A new owner renamed the premises **The Rosary** and it was later called **Century House**. The northern part of the building continued to be used during and after the war by Arthur Vincent who ran it as a cycle and radio shop where he also sold torches and batteries, and customers would come from villages as far away as Browston to have their radio accumulators re-charged there..

The whole premises became a private home in 1956, and by 1981 its history was acknowledged under the title of **Crown House**. After extensive modern modifications, including the fitting of dormer windows, the property now comprises two separate homes at numbers 9 and 9A The Street.

No photographs have come to light of **The Crown** when it was a pub. The 1949 view of The Street shows it on the far left, still in unaltered condition and with the annex in use as a shop. Directly opposite, across the road, stands the large barn which was once one of the mill's outbuildings. The modern photograph shows that this now forms part of a domestic property known as The Willows, where until quite recently remains of an old brick kiln could be seen in the garden.

Ocean Cottages This sturdy-looking small terrace at the bottom of The Street was built towards the end of the 1800s. It appears on the original Ordnance Survey map of 1882 and was probably newly-built at the time. Prior to this, the land on which **Ocean Cottages** stands was described as an 'arable pightle' which, earlier in the 18th century, had been owned by Barney Bristow, licensee of the Malt and Hops. Ocean Cottages are reported to have been built by Benjamin Jackson junior, the nephew of the former brickyard owner of the same name who died in 1862. During the 1850s the younger Benjamin Jackson was licensee at The Plough, but he was a trained bricklayer and may subsequently have returned to his old trade. Although Ocean Cottages consists of three houses, only two front doors are visible when viewed from The Street, the entrance to no. 1 being at the side. There was once a smoke house in the grounds of no. 1 but this has long since disappeared.

The photographs of **Ocean Cottages** were taken in 1958 and 2014, and in the intervening period a revision of the first floor bedroom arrangements appears to have taken place.

Ellen Cottages This terrace of three cottages probably dated from the early 1800s. The first recorded owner is William Osborn in 1837; he lived in one of them and rented the other two out. The 1851 census finds him still in residence, now aged 62, while his brickmaker son John (aged 29) lived in another with his wife and child (they eventually had nine). The third cottage was then occupied by farm labourer John Wilson (30) with his wife and five children, and he was still there in 1871. Later generations of the Osborns were at **Ellen Cottages** when the 1911 census was taken, and over the ensuing years many tenants came and went.

By 1960 Lothingland Rural District Council owned the property and decided to replace it by a modern block of three houses containing all modern facilities. **Ellen Cottages** were demolished in 1968/69 and the new houses were constructed shortly afterwards, slightly to the south and facing Church Road. The '**Ellen Cottages**' name plaque was rescued by Patrick Paul and can still be found built into the wall surrounding Mill House.

The 1960 photograph shows the tower of the mill peeping above the roof top of **Ellen Cottages** before the current conical cap was placed on it. The modern council houses were photographed in 2003, and across the road can be seen Ocean Cottages next to the Blacksmith's Corner site where the smithy used to be.

Blacksmith's Corner and The Street in about 1908, showing also Ellen Cottages and the Mill House. This is taken from a Durrant postcard with Durrant himself posing on the right hand side of the group of three.

Although only a comparatively small village, Blundeston had two active blacksmith's shops for much of the 19th century and into the early 20th. While William Boyce was busy in his smithy midway along The Street, James Candler ran a competing business situated on the corner of The Street and Church Road (then often referred to as Church Lane or Somerleyton Road). Candler lived in the house adjacent to the smithy which, in 1851, he shared with his wife and four children and also a lodger, John Walker, a journeyman blacksmith from Leicestershire. The house also served as the village post office, and both it and the smithy, plus other adjoining properties, were owned by wheelwright James Cleveland.

In 1856 Candler's wife died at the age of 47, and by 1861 he had re-married and moved away from Blundeston. He was replaced by William Boyce junior, the second blacksmith of this name to serve the village. At the time his father William was still active at Blundeston's other smithy although responsibility for running it now rested with William Boyce junior's younger brother Samuel. It is not known if the two brothers worked in competition or in harmony with each other at this time.

A third William Boyce, born in 1859, duly entered the blacksmith scene. The second William Boyce died in February 1894 and the two blacksmith shops were run henceforth by Samuel and William (the third). It was the latter who sold family properties in The Street to make way for the new Methodist Chapel, and who closed the nearby smithy in about 1908, perhaps coinciding with his uncle Samuel's retirement from the business.

The third William Boyce with his family outside their cottage adjoining the smithy in about 1904. An archway led directly from the front garden to the blacksmith's shop. The house, with its unusual arched window, faced on to Church Road. From the end of the front garden the roof of Ocean Cottages is just visible above the smithy..

The side of the smithy is plastered with adverts for local events. It was only a very short walk from the heat of the smithy to the Crown for a pint of beer!

Thereafter the single smithy at what was known as **Blacksmith's Corner** continued to function, although the Boyce family's connection with it ended in April 1929 when the third William Boyce died at the age of 70. It was subsequently run by the Lound blacksmith Charles Jarvis and from about 1937 by Harold Jarvis, joined when required by a Mr. Horner. In its later days, with trade diminishing, it opened only as required, and complete closure came in 1946. In 1968/69 the old properties were demolished and the modern house known as 7 Church Road was erected on the site.

MARKET LANE

No housing existed alongside the eastern end of Market Lane until the early 20th century when **Valley House** was built in 1901 by James Horn. The younger man in the photograph is thought to be his son Herbert. The property included three acres of land on which fruit was grown. James Horn died in January 1910 aged 81 but Herbert continued to live there with his family until at least 1939. Walter Lewis bought it to continue the market garden business, and a large greenhouse was constructed in 1952.

A later generation of the Lewis family still lives there and maintains the market garden tradition. Surplus flowers and fruit are still sold at the gate, and sticks of rhubarb were on offer when **Valley House** was photographed in 2015.

Jay's Cottage (below) stood until 1971 where the modern chalet bungalow **Holbeck** is now sited. Along with a semi-detached property next door, it belonged to the Woods family of Blundeston Hall, and at the tithe survey in 1837 it was occupied by Henry Barnard, a journeyman carpenter, who was the tenant until his death in May 1866. Edward Jay, a farm labourer, lived there with his wife Mary and family from at least 1901 and his name lingered on after he died in 1927 at the age of 83 as the property continued to be known as **Jay's Cottage**, At the outbreak of war the tenant was Sarah Horn, a holiday camp cleaner, and from 1943 the Fountain family lived there until the cottage fell into disuse. The photograph of its rather weatherworn frontage dates from its later days.

The modern photograph of **Holbeck** shows, to the left of it and set further back from the roadway, the substantially-built semi-detached houses known as **The Hall Cottages**. These were constructed by the Woods family in 1905 to replace the earlier pair of houses which had stood on the same plot of land but much closer to Market Lane and in 1851 housed the families of Robert Margetson and James Sleater, both farm labourers who were probably employed on the Blundeston Hall estate.

The 1842 map shows a cluster of cottages standing in isolation from the rest of the village at the far end of **The Loke,** which stretches in a northerly direction from Market Lane and, even in the 21st century, remains largely unmetalled. Four families were housed in three distinct buildings, the most westerly of which comprised a pair of semi-detached cottages. The centre one of these three was just a modest property, as this undated photograph shows, and in the mid-1800s it was owned by prominent local farmer James Crow. In 1851 it was inhabited by Samuel Balls, a farm labourer, plus his wife and four children and a 22 year old lodger Charles Gooch, who was recorded in later years as a fisherman.

In the 1851 census the roadway leading to these cottages is shown as **Mariner's Loke** and in 1871 as **Rivett's Loke**, and it was still referred to by the latter name at the start of the second world war. In recent times it has simply been known as **The Loke.**

The same cottage, photographed in 2007, still exists although a single-storey extension at the front has resulted in the front door being transferred to the back. Owned for many years by jobbing builder Ralph Whitehead, the cottage had the unusual name of **Echo Sierra**, reflecting its owner's interest in amateur radio. Today it carries the equally unusual name of **Bedlam.**

The semi-detached cottages still survive, and the roof of them can be seen to the left of **Echo Sierra**, but the other – which was located on the right hand side of The Loke – was demolished at some time in the 1960s and no trace of it can be seen today.

Back in the 1800s the track continued across the next three fields to serve two remote cottages located on what was then known as Loke Heath, close to the wide track which still exists today as a public footpath across How Heath to emerge into Lound Road via Poplar Farm. One of these cottages was situated almost straight ahead from where the photograph was taken close to Brickhill Wood, and the other one – apparently a semi-detached property – was some way to the west of this near the big sand pit which can be easily identified to this day even though it is overgrown with trees. Both cottages were owned in 1837 by James Crow and various farm labourers and their families occupied them over the years, notable among which were members of the Gooch family who were present in **The Loke** and on the Heath for some four decades. It is not known when these two old cottages were pulled down, but they may not have lasted into the 20th century.

The vista when viewed from the sharp bend in Market Lane has changed in quite recent times from rural to semi-urban. The only building to be seen near at hand in the older photograph is the substantial barn which was once part of **Holly Farm** and was in the process of being converted into a house by Dennis Osborn in 1981. Today other properties surround it including the terrace of four houses known as Osborn Cottages which were built in a sympathetic style to that of the former barn in 2005.

To the north of Market Lane close to the bend in the road was the substantial but rather plain looking house known latterly as **The Nurseries.** The house was built on farm land once belonging to Gidney Booth in about 1880 and contemporary maps indicate that there were once many mature trees in the grounds. At the beginning of World War I the site was turned over to market gardening and substantial greenhouses were constructed, some of which can be seen to the left of the house. James Jermy ran a market gardening business from here for about 40 years. After standing empty for many years the house was finally demolished in 1998 and four years later a strip of land adjoining Market Lane became part of a small housing estate when Pickwick Way was built. In 2007 further houses were constructed where the greenhouses had once stood.

The undated photograph taken close to the bend in the road looks north-eastwards across Rivett's Pond towards **The Nurseries** which stands well back from Market Lane behind a small tree screen. On the right can be seen the **Holly Farm barn** as it looked in the days before it was converted into a house.

From the same viewpoint, Holly Farm barn is seen in 2015, as are the houses created in 2002 fronting Market Lane and Pickwick Way on the plot where **The Nurseries** once stood. Rivett's Pond. in the foreground, was thoroughly dredged – along with Peto's Pond – in 2002 using a Heritage Lottery Fund grant.

Holly Farmhouse faced on to Market Lane a few yards south of the old barn and various outbuildings. Its first recorded owner was James Crow in 1837, who farmed several unconnected tracts of land both in the vicinity of Market Lane and on How Heath. By 1871 the property was in the hands of William Palmer Rivett who was 48 years old at the time and was recorded as employing seven men and two boys to work the farm which had now expanded to 200 acres.

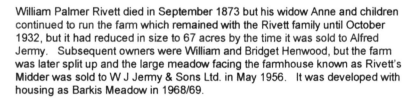

William Palmer Rivett died in September 1873 but his widow Anne and children continued to run the farm which remained with the Rivett family until October 1932, but it had reduced in size to 67 acres by the time it was sold to Alfred Jermy. Subsequent owners were William and Bridget Henwood, but the farm was later split up and the large meadow facing the farmhouse known as Rivett's Midder was sold to W J Jermy & Sons Ltd. in May 1956. It was developed with housing as Barkis Meadow in 1968/69.

Holly Farmhouse was a substantial four bedroom property and its final tenant in the 1960s and 70s was farmhand John Norman who, along with his wife Ansalena, provided a home for fostered children. It eventually stood unoccupied for many years and became ever more dilapidated. It was demolished in 1984 and three large modern houses were built on the site.

Orchard Cottage was thought to be possibly the oldest cottage in Blundeston. Documents relating to it date back to 1637 and there is reference to a cottage in this location in 1710. It was part of a small 15 acre estate which, by 1837, was farmed by Gidney Booth. Apart from **Orchard Cottage** itself, and its yard and outbuildings, there were six fields or 'pightles' with names such as The Spong (which lay alongside the footpath between Market Lane and The Street), with Home Close beyond it and Market Lane Pightle beyond that.

Gidney Booth died in June 1870 at the age of 65 and the property subsequently changed hands a number of times. Various plots were sold off over the years including all the land facing on to The Street. In 1920 Captain 'Lucky' Lockwood MC moved in and was described in 1923 as a poultry farmer and in 1929 as a fruit grower, and he was last recorded there in 1933. At that time the cottage was called **The Retreat**. For a while it was lived in by Hubert Leslie McMichael of McMichael Radios, and in November 1938 it was purchased by Colonel A J Norman and his wife Bertha for use as a holiday home. In 1950 the cottage was remodelled and extended, and at about that time an old barn in front of it was converted into living accommodation to make it possible for the Normans to have 'live in' help.

After the deaths (in London) of both of the Normans, **Orchard Cottage** and its grounds stood empty for several years and by the beginning of the 1990s had become very dilapidated. An effort was made in 1997 to have **Orchard Cottage** 'listed' to prevent it from being demolished but this was unsuccessful and in 1998 both the cottage and the barn were pulled down. The extensive orchard surrounding them was removed, and the land – together with the former site of The Nurseries adjacent to it – was developed with houses and bungalows as Micawber Mews and Pickwick Way.

The top photograph, possibly taken between the wars, shows Orchard cottage in its idyllic setting with roses around the door and surrounded by mature trees. The well has a pantile roof to match the cottage, as does the roof on the side of the barn which stands in front of the cottage.

The aerial photograph shows the location of Orchard Cottage with the converted barn standing in front of it close to the sharp bend in Market Lane where nowadays Pickwick Way branches off. The pond and Barkis Meadow are visible on the left, and at the top can be seen some of the homes built on a large area of land sold to W. Tubby in 1964 and developed as Orchard Close and Orchard Lane.

Photos taken in November 1997 (lower left) show Orchard Cottage and the converted barn in their derelict condition shortly before demolition. The extension to the eastern end of Orchard Cottage added in 1950 and the substantial greenhouse which was a feature at the western end can be clearly seen.

The photograph (bottom right) was taken during the construction of the new housing estate. At the time the old barn was still in existence and is on the left of the picture, but Orchard Cottage itself had been demolished and its site was occupied by the newly constructed house and garage forming 4 Micawber Mews. The fully completed detached house on the right is 2 Micawber Mews.

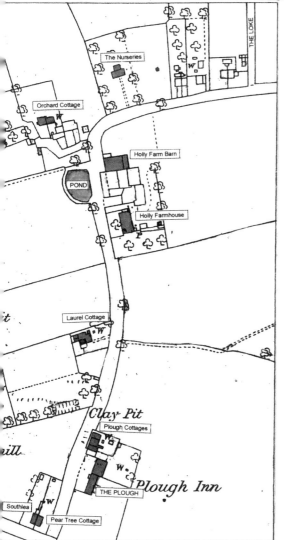

These two views of Market Lane were taken from the same spot but with more than a century separating them. The earlier picture dates from about 1910 and the other from 2015. Common to both are the two semi-detached houses with unusual sloping roofs to their dormer windows; they are named **Great Expectations** and **Barkis** in recognition of Charles Dickens' connection with the Plough Inn next door. The houses, which were quite new at the time of the earlier photograph, were clearly influenced in their design by the 'arts and crafts' movement then in vogue, with the result that they bear little resemblance to the traditional village property, and even today manage to look newer than they really are.

Only the roof and chimneys of The Plough can be glimpsed in the earlier scene, the bulk of the building being set back from the roadway and hidden from view by Plough Cottages which were demolished in the 1950s to provide additional space for car parking. The pink-fronted Plough and its pub sign are in full view in the later photograph.

Closer to the camera, the entrance to Laurel Cottage can be seen on the right in both photographs, as can the start of the footpath on the left where a woman and child are standing in the older photograph. This path still crosses the fields to emerge close to where the two old cottages once stood on the track leading from Market Lane to Blundeston Hall. Today housing reaches right up to the footpath which runs alongside Seymour House. The provision of a pavement means that the roadway is narrower at this point now than it was a century ago.

The map of Market Lane shows the properties that existed in about 1885 with those mentioned in the text shown in colour. A complex of farm buildings is shown next to Orchard Cottage which may not have survived long after the map was drawn, and the barn to the south of the cottage which was later converted into living accommodation does not appear to have been built at this time. The presence of a well in the grounds of various properties is denoted by the letter W.

Laurel Cottage as it appeared in the early 1900s with its substantial greenhouse reaching up as high as the eaves of the house, plus various outbuildings. This is probably the same building that was recorded as existing on this site in the 1830s, which at the time was owned by William Richmond but rented out to James Slater. William Richmond, a journeyman brickmaker, also owned the Plough Cottages and lived in one of them. Both properties were in the Richmond family for many years, and by the time of the 1851 census William had moved across the road to live in **Laurel Cottage**. He was still there at the time of the 1871 census and he died in April 1879 at the age of 82.

Although much altered, **Laurel Cottage** still stands today in its secluded spot on the western side of Market Lane, and although the big greenhouse was removed many decades ago, the outline of the original domestic structure can still be discerned.

Seymour House was built across the road from Laurel Cottage, probably in the 1920s judging by its styling. At the outbreak of war it was the home of John Hopley, an under gardener, but in the early 1940s it was lived in by Philip Pearce, the village coal merchant, following his marriage in 1941 to widow Sarah Horn, previously of Jay's Cottage in Market Lane. A later resident was Lily Youngman whose husband had been one of the longest serving licensees at the nearby Plough Inn, having been recorded there for more than two decades from about 1916 onwards. Lily had taken over as licensee after his death and did not retire until the 1950s. She died in February 1964 at the age of 85. **Seymour House**, which had stood unoccupied for a long time, still displayed many of its original features when photographed in semi-derelict condition in March 2007.

Seymour House was sold and considerably enlarged in 2008, but the core of the old property still survives beneath a much altered exterior. Fortunately a modern styling was not adopted and as a result much of the original character of **Seymour House** has been invoked in the rebuilding. The original name plaque was retained and is incorporated in the front gable.

This innocuous-looking building stood until quite recently close to the southern end of Market Lane facing The Plough. It was built as a slaughterhouse for pigs and was owned by Robert Woodcock who was first recorded as a pork butcher in Blundeston in 1916 and remained active in this trade through the inter-war years. The wooden buildings behind the brick-built slaughterhouse included a stables associated with the butchery business, and it was probably in one of these that Robert Woodcock and his staff made sausages, lard and brawn. The slaughterhouse had long ceased to be used as such when it was photographed in 1996. The wooden buildings were demolished in about 1998 followed by the slaughterhouse itself in 2013. A detached house now occupies the site.

Robert Woodcock lived in the left hand one of these two Victorian cottages standing just inside Short Road at its junction with Market Lane. Nowadays this is named **Southlea** and the one next door is **Pear Tree Cottage**, and the slaughterhouse and its associated buildings were situated immediately behind these two cottages. Before they were built, the land had been recorded as a 'garden' which in 1837 was owned by 83 year old John Moore who lived across the road in an old cottage next to The Plough.

A single storey annexe to **Southlea** served as Robert Woodcock's butcher's shop, from which he also distributed milk that he obtained from Poplar Farm. In addition, Mrs. Woodcock provided a room in the main house for visiting doctors. After the butchery business closed the former shop was converted into living accommodation.

The photograph above shows **Southlea** and **Pear Tree Cottage** as they appeared in 1998 with the low-roofed, one-time butcher's shop now serving as living accommodation. At the time **Pear Tree Cottage** still retained its original austere front door and porch, but these were lost in 2000 when the cottage was modernised. Also in view are two of the council houses erected on the site of allotments in the mid-1940s.

Rebuilding and expansion of **Southlea** included removal of the external rendering and revealed some of the original patterned brickwork. This work was finished in 2014. The bricked-up outline of the doorway to the old butcher's shop can just be seen on the side of the building.

The two cottages as they appeared in 2015. Modernisation of the council house nearest to these is also evident. The new house built on the site of the old slaughterhouse can be seen behind **Pear Tree Cottage.**

The most prominent and best-known building in Market Lane is **The Plough Inn** which even today draws customers from far and wide. Iron numerals on the exterior appear to date it from 1701 and tethering rings from its days as a coaching inn are visible on the front wall. The earliest recorded owner is John Sayers Bell, a long established Gorleston brewer, and it was one of twenty public houses sold by Bell's Brewery to Steward & Patteson of Norwich in 1866. Just over a century later, in February 1967, Steward & Patteson's business passed to Watney Mann who closed the Norwich brewery in January 1970.

Over the years **The Plough** was run by many licensees who, in earlier times, also pursued other trades which probably indicates that the inn was not enough by itself to provide them with an adequate living. Licensees of inns such as **The Plough** were badly hit by an 1830 Act of Parliament allowing anyone to open a beer house on payment of a licence fee which resulted in two beer houses being set up in The Street soon afterwards in direct competition with **The Plough**. John Skinner, who was licensee from at least 1837 into the 1840s also worked as a butcher; William Scurrell in the 1850s was a shoemaker and Benjamin Jackson junior a bricklayer. William Marjoram in the 1860s was a butcher and John Gough, in the 1870s, a butcher and gardener. Licensees after John Gough included Mrs. Frances Marjoram, Oliver Moore, Charles Aldridge and George Bolton, and stability did not come until about 1916 when William Youngman became licensee, after which the Yougman family remained there through to the 1950s.

The Plough probably owes its survival and continued popularity to having been mentioned by Charles Dickens as the hostelry from which Barkis, the carrier, set out in the novel 'David Copperfield', and long may this continue to be so.

The Plough, photographed (above) in the early 1900s, looks a little run-down and in need of a coat of paint. The two Plough Cottages are on the left with what appears to be a warehouse and hay loft adjoining them, and a horse trough standing alongside. At the 1871 census the cottages were owned by William Richmond junior (who died in 1879). One was lived in by his carpenter son Aaron with his wife and four children, and the other by the family of John Lydamore, the brother of Aaron Richmond's wife Kezla.

A few years later (lower photograph) the inn and its adjoining cottages look little changed but the roof line of the newly erected cottages (today known as **Barkis** and **Great Expectations**) is clearly visible. Across the road an early motor car stands outside the semi-detached cottages which today form a single property known as **Virginia Cottage**.

This photo probably dates from the 1930s by which time the bricked-up window aperture above the doorway was used to advertise **The Plough's** Barkis connection, as it still is today.

Demolition of the Plough cottages in about 1955 was accompanied by considerable alterations and improvements to the interior of the public house including the creation of its Dickens Lounge and the installation of oak wall benches, oak tables and oak wheelback chairs designed by the licensee at the time, Stanley Reed. This view of the exterior was taken in 2015.

At one time this pair of old cottages stood adjacent to The Plough on its southern side. In 1841 they were owned by John Moore aged 85 who occupied one of them himself; the other was lived in by 27 years old Mary Patrick and her younger sister Emily. Both remained spinsters and in 1851 Mary was described as a pauper and Emily as a needlewoman. Their brother John – a farm labourer and fisherman – then lived next door with his family. The Patrick sisters were still there in 1871, but the cottages do not appear on an 1882 map and had presumably been demolished by then.

BLUNDESTON & FLIXTON VILLAGE HALL.

HALL LANE

The Village Hall. The Blundeston and Flixton branch of the Women's Institute was formed in 1922 and one of their first major projects was to build a village hall. A loan had to be set up to fund its construction and supporters paid six pence (2½p in today's money) per brick to help towards the £250 cost. Construction work by H Taylor was completed in 1926. The hall was designed so that, if it proved a failure, it could be easily converted into two cottages. However it was an immediate success and soon became the centre for a variety of village social activities. The running of the hall was subsequently passed to the Parish Council, and during World War II soldiers were billeted there.

As a result of the rapid expansion of the village in the 1960s and 70s, it was decided to modernise and enlarge the hall. The area to the left of the entrance doorway was doubled in size and a new kitchen was provided. The cost of £12,000 was met by fund-raising and a grant from Waveney District Council, plus an increase of 4½p on the parish precept for a limited period of two years. The rebuilt premises were opened in 1981 and present at the re-opening was 80 years old Mabel Hathaway who had been one of the Women's Institute members responsible for its original construction back in 1926.

The receipt of a lottery grant of £73,400 enabled Gilbert Builders to begin further reconstruction work in July 1998. The roof was raised to accommodate the whole premises under a single span; new toilets and storage facilities were built and gas heating was installed. Although a large new porch was added, the work was carried out sympathetically retaining the old-style appearance of the hall. Its re-opening on 12th December 1998 was carried out by Patrick Paul who had been a member of the Parish Council for over 40 years. In 2008 a further £18,000 was spent on a replacement floor.

New name signs were erected in 2015

50

The tennis court, Hall Lane
Before World War II there was a grass tennis court near the village hall, but during the war soldiers who were billeted in the hall parked their vehicles on the grass and after the war ended the court was not reinstated. In 1970 a group of villagers raised £1,500 and constructed a concrete tennis court on the site. Holiday chalets were donated and made into a pavilion and the court was opened in 1973. Due to vandalism the pavilion was removed in 1996 and the court was resurfaced in 2001 at a cost of £12,000. Taken in 1996, this view of a corner of the court also shows the back of the village hall with its old roofline.

Heddon's Piece Many years ago this plot of land, in common with the site on which the village hall stands, belonged to the church and formed part of the glebe land. In 1945 it was offered back to the church by Mrs. Dorothy Heddon for use as a 'Children's Corner' in memory of her late husband. The Reverend Bernard Godfrey suggested, instead, that it should be given to the Parish Council to which she agreed. The original playground equipment, shown in this photograph from the 1980s, comprised swings, a roundabout and a seesaw of types widely used in children's playgrounds throughout the country, which will be familiar to many readers.

In 2009 an attractive and innovative new layout was designed for **Heddon's Piece** which has proved to be a great success.

The trend within recent times has been for various small bungalows built in the village during the 1930s and later to be extended in size or even completely demolished and replaced by larger properties. **Grandora** is one such bungalow that has been altered almost out of all recognition.

Horatio Taylor, the son of the landlord at The Crown, carried out much building work in and around Blundeston in the 1930s. He built the next door property to **Grandora** called Copperfield (another modest bungalow since considerably enlarged) where he lived with his wife Gertrude and daughter Violet, a shorthand typist. Violet married Frank Smith, a Canadian serviceman who came to this country in World War II, and Frank worked with his father-in-law to build **Grandora** for Violet and himself, where they lived all their married lives. Horatio Taylor died in February 1957 at the age of 71. The photograph of **Grandora** taken in 1994 shows how this modest bungalow once looked.

After Violet and Frank passed away **Grandora** was sold and considerably enlarged. The later picture (above) was taken in 2003 before the new trees and shrubs on the Millennium Green had grown to hide most of it from view. Only the distinctive bay windows at the front survive as a reminder of how the bungalow once looked. In 2012 permission was given for a small care home to be added.

Another typical 1930s bungalow in Hall Lane was **Fairwind** (right). In the 1930s it was lived in by Stanley Rudd, the local haulage contractor, but it subsequently became the long-term home of Dulcie and Roy Knights. This photograph of it was taken in 2011. Dulcie lived into her nineties, and subsequent to her death in 2012 the property was sold. In 2013 the old bungalow was completely demolished and the current fine new house was put in its place by Badger Building.

Construction of the new property was completed in 2014, but fortunately the old name of **Fairwind** has been retained as a reminder of earlier days.

When viewed from the garden of **Fairwind** in 1964 Hall Lane still bore a semi-rural aspect and was much narrower than it is today. In times gone by the meadows on both sides had been part of the large Blundeston Hall estate which, in the mid 19th century was owned jointly by the Woods brothers, John Jex, Thomas and William. The land on the right, which was sold off first, was once known as Fritton Hall Yard. Soon to be built upon, the field on the left was referred to in earlier times as Plough Close.

This view shows the same meadow in 1965 after the builders had moved in and typifies the rapid expansion of the village at that time. Eight new properties were built including four identical chalet bungalows. The one most advanced in its construction, with its roof timbers being put into place, is known today as **Aventura**.

In the half-century since their completion, the new residences in Hall Lane have inevitably mellowed into their background and each one has taken on a character of its own as various embellishments have been added to the extent that some now barely resemble their original condition. The chalet bungalows photographed in this 2014 scene are **Brackenfield**, **Tranquil** and **Aventura**.

In times gone by county police constabularies were organised on a village basis and in the 19th century most villages of any size had its own police station house staffed by a uniformed constable. Blundeston was no exception and the first recorded policeman in the village was Robert Jefferies in 1855. Maps dating from the later part of the 19th century show 39 The Street as being the police station, and the constable living there in 1871 was Charles Dix who originated from Dorset. He was still there in 1885 but by 1891 had retired from the force to become a pork butcher and was succeeded by Alfred Flurry.

A succession of police constables followed in the 20th century who would have occupied the fine new police house and station in Hall Lane after it was constructed in about 1930. At the outbreak of war the resident police constable was Roland Chipperield, but the longest occupant of the post appears to have been Peter Mounser who was the village policeman from 1965 until his retirement in September 1988. After PC Andy Green vacated the house in 1991 it was put up for sale. Village police houses were no longer considered economic, and police patrols since then have been carried out in cars.

The photograph (above) shows the former police house as it appeared when viewed from the bend in Hall Lane just north of the T-junction in 1996. The orange pipes in the foreground, and the blue compressor trailer, indicate that a public gas supply is belatedly being installed in Blundeston.

Part of the police house's large garden was sold separately, and the view (below) taken from much the same location shows the modern house **Appletrees** which now stands on the site, hiding the old police house from view. A new boundary hedge has been established which is set further back than the old one and considerably improves the site-line for northbound traffic on Hall Lane.

A bird's eye view of the southern part of the village in the nineteen-eighties. Prominent in the foreground is the T-junction where Hall Lane meets Lowestoft Road and Hall Road. All the houses and bungalows in Hall Lane can be identified from **Grandora**, at the top, to the **police house** and its large garden at the bottom. St. Mary's church is visible at the top left of the photograph. The most recent new building at the time, which was then nearing completion, was **Hall Farm bungalow**, facing the T-junction and accessed from Lowestoft Road.

As a reminder of the old days on local farms, this replica hay wain has stood immobile on the Hall Lane corner since 2014 celebrating 'Blundeston in Bloom'.

LOWESTOFT ROAD

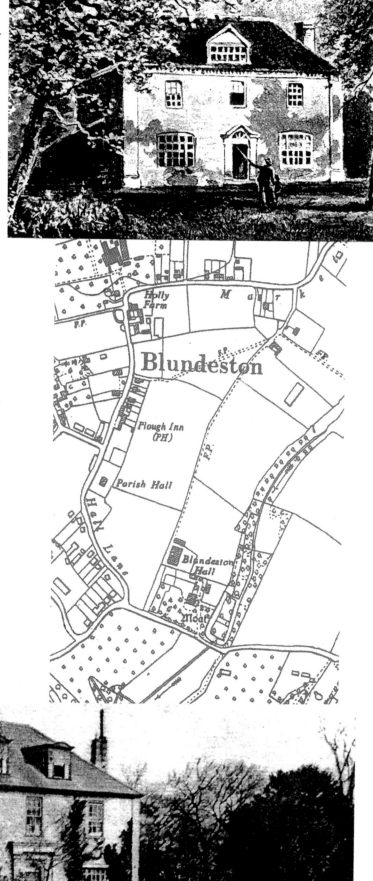

Blundeston Hall is believed to have been built in the late 1660s for Admiral Sir Thomas Allin on the site of an earlier building the remains of which can still be seen in the cellars of the present house.   The site is an ancient one identified with the medieval manor of Blundeston, and about 45 metres to the east of the house is a large 13th century water-filled moat registered as a scheduled monument by Historic England although no buildings now remain on the moated site.

Sir Thomas Allin was Lord of the Manor of Blundeston, but he moved to the grander Somerleyton Hall in 1672 and later occupiers included the Luson family in the early 18th century.   In about 1769 the estate was purchased by Robert Woods, a farmer and corn miller from Somerleyton, and the Woods family continued to be owners throughout the 19th century during which they were prominent landowners in Blundeston.   At the time of the 1851 census the estate extended to 229 acres and 12 men were employed to work it.

The titular owner of the estate seldom lived there, but over the years **Blundeston Hall** was lived in by various other members of the Woods family.   However at the time of the 1871 census it was occupied by John Godbold and his family as caretakers with Godbold acting as farm bailiff. The Woods' main house was now at Llandaff Hall, Cardiff, and **Blundeston Hall** gradually became neglected.   After major renovations in 1895/96 Thomas Hardwick Woods JP moved in and ownership of the estate passed to him by deed of gift in January 1897.   A fine horseman and equestrian judge, he became nicknamed by the locals as 'Hardup' Woods, perhaps because the family fortunes were now in decline, causing the Hall and its contents to be put up for sale in 1916.   Thomas Hardwick Woods moved initially to Felixstowe and died in Devon in 1947.

The remaining property was purchased by Spencer Arnold for £1,687, and after his death in May 1935 **Blundeston Hall** changed hands six times prior to being purchased by its present owner, Stephen George, in September 1995.

Top illustration   Blundeston Hall was built in the 'Queen Anne' style.   This view of it probably dates from the mid-1800s,
Centre   The moat is shown on this 1950s map along with the stream feeding it from the north and the run-off channel to the lake at its southern end.   The old footpath linking Blundeston Hall with Market Lane is also clearly marked.
Bottom   An early 20th century view shows the alterations made in 1895/96 including the revised dormers, the more substantial front door and porch and the cappings above the downstairs windows.

A fine view of **Blundeston Lodge** could be had from across the lake. The lake was fed by water channelled under Lowestoft Road from the moat at Blundeston House, and it left the lake at its south-west corner to flow to Flixton House and decoy. The 1837 tithe survey names two small islands situated at the western end of the lake as Long Island and Duncan's Island.

The foundation stone for **Blundeston prison** was laid by the Rt. Hon. R.A. Butler on 12th May 1961 and the new prison complex was officially opened by the Rt. Hon. Henry Brooke on 22nd July 1963. It was the first of 22 so-called 'New Wave' prisons and the first purpose-built prison to be opened since Victorian times. Initially a maximum security unit, it contained four T-shaped cell blocks built to a new design with each one accommodating 75 inmates within what were effectively individual communities. After several early escapes, an additional perimeter fence was built, the final arrangement being an outer 'modesty' wall enclosing two 5.3m (17ft 6ins) high mesh fences topped with barbed wire and with a no-man's-land in between. There was a single watch tower.

The prison land originally comprised some 250 acres and included a farm which undertook intensive piggery and arable crop production. There were various workshops and training courses. Additional buildings were constructed over the years including two more cell blocks in 1975, and the prison's security rating was downgraded. In 2001/2 the Home Office sold about 55 acres of prison land including the whole of the lake, the latter being purchased by a local syndicate who use it for fishing.

Despite some £10million having been spent on improvements within the past three years, the surprise announcement was made on 4th September 2013 by the Secretary of State for Justice that **Blundeston prison** was to be closed as soon as possible as an economy measure. It was vacated remarkably quickly, with a final closing ceremony taking place on 23rd December 2013.

This photograph shows the proximity of the lake to the prison, and some prisoners could see the lake from their cell windows. The four original T-shaped accommodation blocks can be clearly seen, with later-built prisoner accommodation sandwiched in between.

The prison and its farm were well hidden from the sight of passing traffic by the mature tree screen along Hall Road, and for obvious security reasons, very few villagers ever got the chance to see inside it apart from those who were employed there.

The upper view shows one of the corridors in the T-blocks with cells lining each side and with a security gate very much in evidence. These were single person cells, although the two later-built blocks contained cells for two or four and were much less austere.

The lower view shows some of the well-equipped indoor recreational facilities which were provided in addition to workshops and other training facilities. Outside sports pitches were available too.

Early in 2016 it was announced that the prison had been sold for redevelopment to local company Badger Building for £3 million, heralding a new era for Blundeston and its residents.

Prison officers and their families came from all over the country in readiness for the opening of the new prison, and provision was made to receive them with the construction of 73 new 3 and 4 bedroom houses to form **Lakeside Rise**. In addition to the spaciously laid-out houses, living quarters were provided for single officers along with a social club building.

Their arrival marked probably the greatest population explosion that Blundeston has ever had, and the number of children on the school roll almost doubled within a few months.

Today most of the **Lakeside Rise** houses are in private ownership.